Cultural Traditions in

China

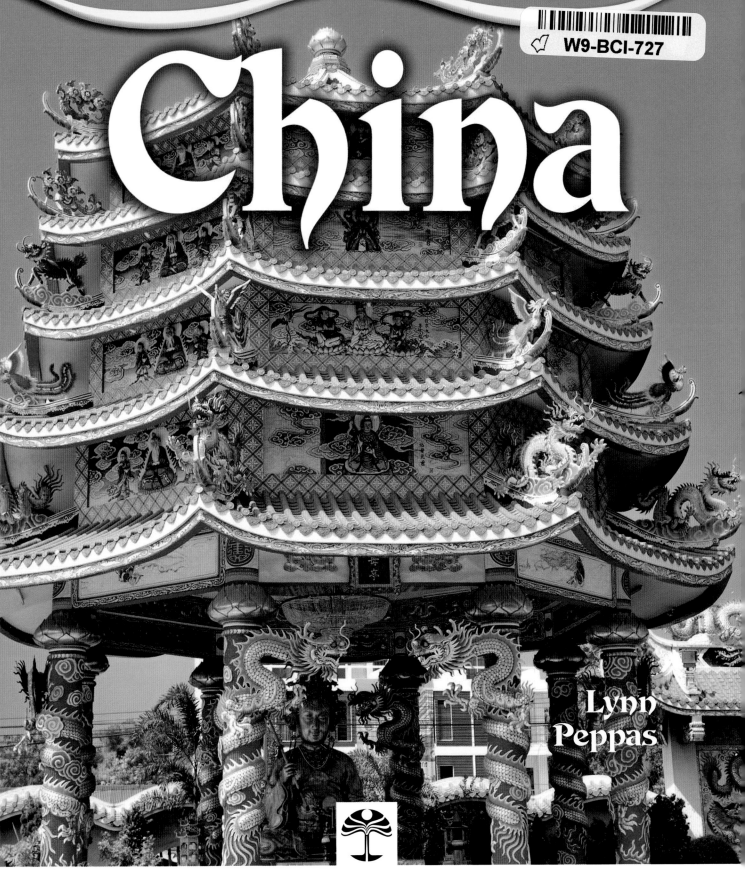

W9-BCI-727

Lynn
Peppas

Crabtree Publishing Company

www.crabtreebooks.com

Crabtree Publishing Company

www.crabtreebooks.com

Author: Lynn Peppas
Publishing plan research and development:
Sean Charlebois, Reagan Miller
Crabtree Publishing Company
Project coordinator: Kathy Middleton
Editor: Adrianna Morganelli
Proofreaders: Kathy Middleton, Crystal Sikkens
Photo research: Allison Napier, Margaret Amy Salter
Design: Margaret Amy Salter
Production coordinator: Margaret Amy Salter
Prepress technician: Margaret Amy Salter
Print coordinator: Katherine Berti

Cover: Lantern Festival (top); Chinese New Year parade (center); traditional moon cake (middle left); FenJiang River Dragon Boat Race in FoShan City, China (bottom left); Chinese ravioli (middle right); Lion dance at a Chinese New Year celebration (bottom right)

Title page: Chinese temple

Photographs:
Dreamstime: Donkeyru: page 17
Shutterstock: cover (middle left and right, top), pages 1, 4–5 (background), 9, 11, 13, 15, 17, 19, 25 (bottom), 27 (bottom), 28, 29; Sergei Bachlakov: cover (center); Marina Ivanova: cover (bottom right); Tan Wei Ming: page 4 (bottom); Cora Reed: page 6; windmoon: cover (bottom left); pages 20–21, 24; BartlomiejMagierowski: page 21 (inset); Jose Antonio Sanchez: page 22; Christophe Testi: page 23; zhaoyan: page 25 (top); Mary416: page 26; Andrea Paggiaro: page 30; Hung Chung Chih: page 31
Thinkstock: pages 4 (top), 5 (top), 8, 10, 12, 14, 16, 18, 27 (top)

Library and Archives Canada Cataloguing in Publication

Peppas, Lynn
    Cultural traditions in China / Lynn Peppas.

(Cultural traditions in my world)
Includes index.
Issued also in electronic format.
ISBN 978-0-7787-7584-3 (bound).--ISBN 978-0-7787-7591-1 (pbk.)

    1. Festivals--China--Juvenile literature. 2. Holidays--China--Juvenile literature. 3. China--Social life and customs--Juvenile literature. I. Title. II. Series: Cultural traditions in my world

GT4883.A2P47 2012   j394.26951   C2012-900666-1

Library of Congress Cataloging-in-Publication Data

Peppas, Lynn.
    Cultural traditions in China / Lynn Peppas.
        p. cm. -- (Cultural traditions in my world)
    Includes index.
    ISBN 978-0-7787-7584-3 (reinforced library binding : alk. paper) --
ISBN 978-0-7787-7591-1 (pbk. : alk. paper) -- ISBN 978-1-4271-7863-3
(electronic pdf) -- ISBN 978-1-4271-7978-4 (electronic html)
    1. Holidays--China--Juvenile literature. 2. Festivals--China--Juvenile literature. 3. China--Social life and customs--Juvenile literature. I. Title.

GT4883.A2P47 2012
394.26951--dc23

                                                    2012003075

Crabtree Publishing Company

www.crabtreebooks.com   1-800-387-7650

Printed in Canada/022012/AV20120110

Published in Canada
Crabtree Publishing
616 Welland Ave.
St. Catharines, ON
L2M 5V6

Published in the United States
Crabtree Publishing
PMB 59051
350 Fifth Avenue, 59th Floor
New York, New York 10118

Published in the United Kingdom
Crabtree Publishing
Maritime House
Basin Road North, Hove
BN41 1WR

Published in Australia
Crabtree Publishing
3 Charles Street
Coburg North
VIC 3058

Contents

Welcome to China

China has more people than any other country on Earth. More than one billion people live there. Most Chinese people speak Mandarin. There are more than 56 different **ethnic** groups in China. The majority, or largest group, is Han Chinese.

Chinese people write in symbols called pictographs. Each pictograph is a whole word.

China is also one of the oldest civilizations on Earth. A civilization is a group of people that live together and share a **culture** and **traditions**. Culture is a group of people's shared history and beliefs. Traditions are ways that people celebrate their culture. Traditions are passed down from **ancestors**.

Yin Yang is a popular symbol in China. It is a symbol of opposites that together make a perfect balance in the world.

Chinese Festivals and Holidays

Chinese New Year is the most important traditional holiday in China. The day of Chinese New Year is different every year because it follows the **lunar** calendar.

Holidays in China are special days that celebrate traditions that have been passed down for hundreds of years. All Chinese people celebrate **national** holidays. Most people living in China get the day off work or school. Many celebrate their culture with festivals. A festival is an event or party where many people get together and share traditions such as eating special foods.

A lunar calendar uses one cycle of the moon to make one month. Chinese New Year starts on a new moon, when you cannot see the moon at all, and runs for about two weeks until the full moon appears.

new moon

full moon

Chinese people use two calendars. They use the Gregorian calendar for everyday activities such as school, work, and appointment dates. This is the same calendar used in North America and around the world. Chinese holidays that fall on the same date every year use the Gregorian calendar. **Ancient** festivals are held on different dates every year because they use the Chinese lunar calendar.

Did You Know?
The Chinese lunar calendar has been used in China for over 2,000 years. The Gregorian calendar has been used there for only one hundred years.

Family Occasions

Family life is very important to the Chinese. Many Chinese households today are made up of parents and children, and sometimes grandparents. Grandparents often care for children while their parents work. Long ago, Chinese parents arranged, or decided, who their children would marry. Today, the custom is that most Chinese people choose their own husband or wife.

In China it is common for many generations of a family to live together in the same household.

An old tradition in China counts a person's age as starting at one year old almost from birth. Today, most Chinese count their age in the usual way. A first birthday is a special celebration. Other important birthdays are at ten years, and then 60, 70, and 80 years.

Did You Know?
Traditional foods for a birthday party are noodles and peaches. Eating these foods means you will enjoy a long life.

Chinese New Year

Dragon and lion dances are held during Chinese New Year. Both are symbols of good luck for the New Year.

Chinese New Year is also called Spring Festival. It is one of the most celebrated festivals in China. People of Chinese heritage also celebrate this festival in other countries such as the United States and Canada. It falls on different days every year between January 21 and February 20. In China, it is called a Golden Week and festivities take place all week long.

Chinese people clean their houses so they are spotless for the New Year. They wear new clothes for the holiday. Firecrackers are lit to scare off evil spirits. Red is a popular color for Chinese New Year. Homes and businesses are dressed with red decorations and flowers. Children are given money for good luck in red envelopes.

Did You Know?
Chinese children stay up late on Chinese New Year's Eve. It is believed that the longer they stay up, the longer their lives will be.

Lantern Festival

Chinese New Year festivities continue for weeks after the New Year. The last day of the festival happens 15 days after the New Year. It is called Feast of the Full Moon or the Lantern Festival. On this day the moon is full and bright in the sky. This day celebrates the light of the sun that warms up the land after the cold winter is through.

Lanterns come in different shapes, colors, and sizes!

Did You Know?
People eat Tangyuan for the Lantern Festival. The balls are made of rice flour and water and look like a white, full moon!

During the Lantern Festival people hang lanterns on the streets and outside their homes. Lanterns are often made of a tough, waxy paper and have a source of light that shines through the paper. Families walk around their neighborhoods and cities at night to look at all the colorful lanterns. It is a beautiful sight!

International Women's Day

International Women's Day is celebrated on March 8 in China as well as many other countries around the world. In China, the first Women's Day was celebrated in 1950. Today, it is a half-day national holiday for women only. That means that most of the women in China get a half day off of work.

Flowers are a thoughtful gift for Women's Day in China.

Husbands and children do nice things for the women in their families. Women are given flowers and presents. It is a day to celebrate the importance of women and all they have done for **equality** for women in China.

Arbor Day

Arbor Day is a day to plant trees. Many countries around the world hold Arbor Day on different dates. Arbor Day in China is always held on March 12. It is held on this day to honor the death of a Chinese man named Sun Yat-sen. He was a doctor who became a leader. He is sometimes called the Father of Modern China.

Did You Know?
If people living in China do not plant trees every year they might have to pay a **fine**.

Yat-sen believed that planting more trees and forests would build a better **environment** for China. The Chinese government made tree-planting a law in 1981. This means that Chinese people from age 11 to age 60 have to plant trees every year.

Young girls in China plant a tree on Arbor Day.

Qing Ming Festival

Qing Ming is a spring festival that celebrates the lives of loved ones who have died. It is sometimes called **Tomb** Sweeping Day. It is an ancient festival that falls on April 4 or 5 every year. It is a national holiday when most people in China get the day off work or school.

Opera is popular in China and is performed during Qing Ming. Chinese operas are plays that feature singing, speaking, acrobatics, and dancing.

Qing Ming is a day to enjoy the spring weather and get outside. It is also a time to visit the gravesites of loved ones. They pray, bring food offerings, and burn candles. The will also burn items such as paper money in the belief that the spirits of the dead will help them get things they want. Children and adults often enjoy the holiday by flying a kite.

Qing Ming is also called Tomb Sweeping Day because people visit and care for the gravesites of loved ones on this day.

May Day

May Day in China is held on the first day of May to celebrate the achievements of workers. It is also called International Labor (or Workers') Day. Many people in China get the day off from work or school. Many countries around the world also celebrate May or Labor Day. Some celebrate on May 1, and others, such as the United States and Canada, celebrate on the first Monday in September.

These women are putting on a martial arts performance in celebration of May Day.

In China, when the May 1 holiday falls on a weekend day, it is bumped backward or forward to the Friday before the weekend, or the Monday after. This is so workers can have a three-day weekend off of work. It is a time to relax and not worry about school or work.

Many people travel or spend time with family and friends on May Day.

Children's Day

Children get their own special holiday in China. Children's Day in China is celebrated on June 1. It is a day to honor children. Children 14 years or younger get the day off from school. Children's Day is celebrated in different countries around the world on different dates. Many other countries' children do not get the day off of school.

Caregivers in China plan special day trips to places such as the zoo on Children's Day.

On Children's Day some schools put together special shows such as dance or art festivals that show their students' **talents**. Relatives and caregivers are invited to see their children's shows. Sometimes children get small gifts on Children's Day.

Did You Know?
Older children in China celebrate Youth Day on May 4. Those older than 14 years get a half day off of school.

23

Dragon Boat Festival

The Dragon Boat Festival is an ancient summer festival that has been held for thousands of years. It is held on the fifth day of the fifth lunar month. It usually falls sometime in June. Long ago, Chinese people believed that dragons lived in rivers and brought rain. They held river festivals to make the dragons happy so they would bring rain for their rice crops.

This festival is known in China as *Duanwu* Festival. It is a national holiday.

On this day in China many watch or take part in dragon boat races. Dragon boats are exactly what they sound like. They are long, narrow boats decorated to look like dragons. Many rowers sit on each side of the boat and use paddles in the water to push the boat forward.

A person in the front of the boat beats a drum to keep the rowers rowing at the same time.

Many people eat a traditional Chinese food called Zongzi during the Dragon Boat Festival. It is rice and beans, or sticky rice, wrapped in bamboo leaves.

Mid-Autumn Day

Mid-Autumn Day is a **harvest** festival. It is called Mid-Autumn Day because it is held in the middle of autumn, or fall. It is sometimes called Moon Festival. It falls on the first full moon in mid-autumn. This means it takes place on different dates in the month of September.

Colorful decorations are on display to celebrate Mid-Autumn Day in Hong Kong, China.

Moon cakes are a traditional food that is eaten on Mid-Autumn Day. They are filled with bean paste, lotus seeds, or egg yolks.

Mid-Autumn Day is a day of thanksgiving for the rice harvest. It is a day off school or work for most people in China. Many go hiking and pack a picnic to enjoy the weather and beauty of autumn.

Chong Yang Festival

Did You Know?
Adults drink wine made from chrysanthemum flowers (above) during Chong Yang Festival.

Chong Yang Festival is held on different dates in the month of October. It is also called the Double Ninth Festival. This is because it is held on the ninth day of the ninth month according to the Chinese lunar calendar. It is not a national holiday.

During the Chong Yang Festival people are supposed to climb to a high place for good luck. Many climb mountains, tall buildings, or go outdoors for a hike. Chrysanthemums are flowers that grow in the autumn. People often decorate with these flowers during this festival.

People in China may climb a pagoda during the Chong Yang Festival. A pagoda is a tall, traditional-style building found throughout China.

National Day

National Day is held on October 1 every year in China. The first National Day was on October 1, 1949. On this day China became a republic. A republic is a country that is ruled by people chosen or elected by the people living in that country. Before China became a republic, it was ruled by **emperors** that were not chosen by the people.

Did You Know?
National Day starts a one-week holiday in China. These special week-long holidays are called Golden Weeks.

On National Day and during Golden Week, adults get the week off of work and children do not go to school. Many families travel during this time to see the sights in China. Many visit Tiananmen Square in Beijing to watch military parades, and see the fireworks display at night.

Bamboo rafting is a popular activity during the National Day holiday.

Glossary

ancestor The relative of a person who was alive before they were born

ancient Something or someone who was around thousands of years ago

culture The beliefs and habits of a group of people

emperor A male ruler or king of a country

environment The natural surroundings of an area

equality To be treated the same as everyone else

ethnic A group of people from a country that share the same language, culture, and beliefs

fine An amount of money charged for breaking a law

harvest The time of year to gather crops that are ripe and ready to be picked

international Having to do with more than one nation or country

lunar Anything that has to do with the moon

national Belonging to everyone in one country or nation

talent The ability to do something really well

tomb The grave that marks where a dead person is buried

tradition Customs or beliefs that are handed down from generation to generation

Index